LITTLE BIG BOOK
PLUS

Table of Contents

My First American Friend **4**
an autobiography by Sarunna Jin
illustrated by Shirley V. Beckes

Sarunna's Journey **24**
a map of Sarunna's route

New Friends, New Words **26**
a language diagram

The More We Get Together **30**
a song from The Raffi Singable Songbook

Meet Sarunna Jin

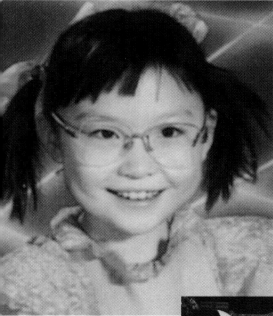

Sarunna Jin wrote *My First American Friend* when she was only eight years old. She had been speaking English for just a little over two years. Sarunna has also written poems, reports, and adventure stories.

Meet Shirley V. Beckes

Shirley Beckes's two best friends are members of her family. They are her husband, David, and her daughter, Jennifer. Their dog, Poindexter, is a new friend!

My First
American Friend

Story by Sarunna Jin
Illustrations by Shirley V. Beckes

HOUGHTON MIFFLIN COMPANY

BOSTON

ATLANTA   DALLAS   GENEVA, ILLINOIS   PALO ALTO   PRINCETON

献给我亲爱的外祖父,外祖母。

To my dearest grandfather and grandmother
with all my love and thanks. — **S.J.**

To my first friend. — **S.B.**

Acknowledgments

For each of the selections listed below, grateful acknowledgment is made for permission
to excerpt and/or reprint original or copyrighted material, as follows:

Text

1 *My First American Friend*, by Sarunna Jin, Illustrated by Shirley V. Beckes. Copyright © 1992 by
Steck-Vaughn Company. Reprinted by permission. **30** "The More We Get Together," traditional.

Illustrations

26–29 Jim Gordon.

Photography

i Banta Digital Group. **ii** Courtesy of Sarunna Jin (tl, cl); courtesy of Shirley V. Beckes (cr, br); Banta
Digital Group (tr, bl). **24** Jean-Marc Truchet/Tony Stone Images (tl); Tony Stone Images (br).
25 Ben Nakayama/Tony Stone Images (l); Rohan/Tony Stone Images (r). **30** Tracey Wheeler.

1997 Impression

Houghton Mifflin Edition, 1996
Copyright © 1996 by Houghton Mifflin Company. All rights reserved.

Printed in the U.S.A.

ISBN 0-395-73168-2

9-B-98 97

I was born in China. When
I was two months old, I went to
live with my grandparents in
a place called Inner Mongolia in China.
This made it possible for my parents to go to school
in a different part of China. They wanted to do this
so that we could all have a better life someday.

Later, my parents went to America to study at a
school called Boston College. It is in the state of
Massachusetts. I stayed with my grandparents in
China. I was happy there with them and my friends.

When I was six years old, my parents asked
me if I would like to join them in America.
I said, "Okay!"

On the morning of my journey to America, I had to get up at five o'clock. My grandma and I traveled by train to Beijing, the capital of China. There we met my aunt, who took us to the airport. Even though I was so young, I was flying to America all by myself!

The trip was a real adventure. I flew from China to Japan, and from Japan to San Francisco in America. From there I flew to New York, where my mom and dad were waiting. We had a happy reunion with hugs and kisses.

Soon after I got to America, I started first grade. I didn't know any English. That made it difficult for me to do everything. I tried to talk with the other children, but we could not understand each other.

No one played with me. Oh, how sad and lonely I was for my friends that I had left behind. I felt especially sad when my mom read a letter from my grandmother. It said that one of my friends in China had knocked on my grandmother's door and asked, "Is Sarunna back yet?" That made me sadder. Then something happened to make me feel better.

I was sitting at my desk during playtime when a girl named Ali came over to play with me. Ali had blue eyes, a pretty smile, and beautiful blonde hair. I had never seen such pretty hair before. Even though I could only speak a little bit of English, Ali and I had lots of fun together. She let me touch her pretty hair.

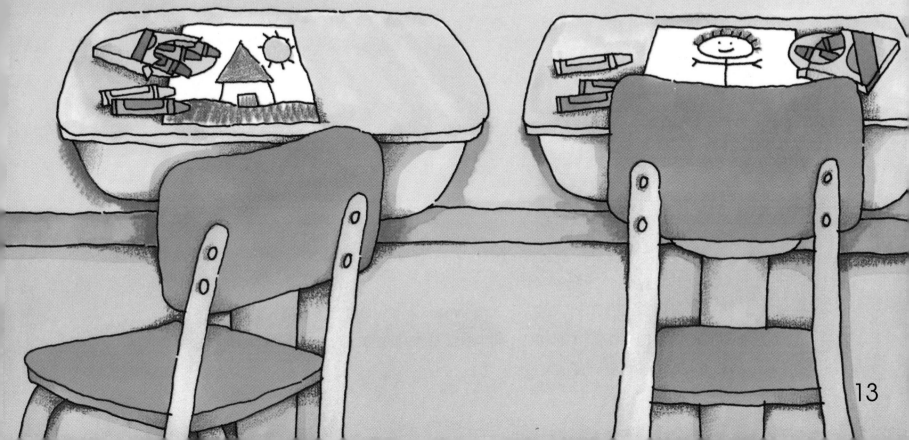

From that day on, we always played together at school. Sometimes we played on the swings. Sometimes we played on the slide.

In the classroom, we built blocks and painted together. Ali and I became best friends and were very happy!

At the end of the year, Ali told me that she was moving to another school. I was sad again because my very best friend was leaving. On the last day of school, we hugged and said good-bye.

In second grade, my English improved a lot. I still had some problems with the language, but I made many new friends.

This year, I am in the third grade, and my English is perfect! I have many friends now, and I'm very happy. But I'll always remember Ali, my first American friend.

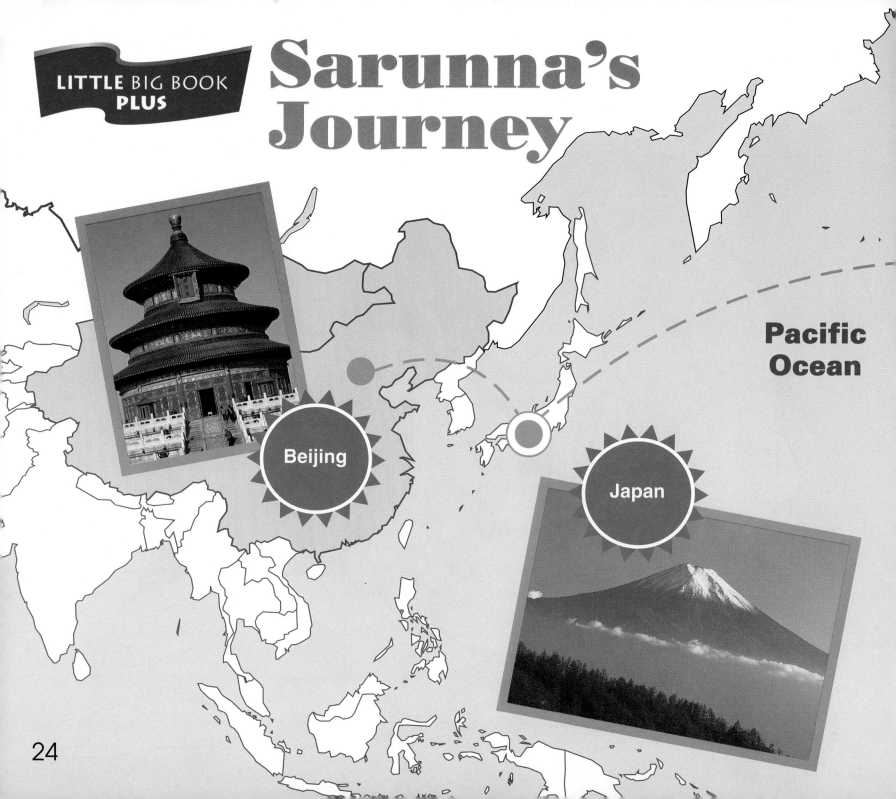

Sarunna's Journey

Pacific
Ocean

Beijing

Japan

New York City

San Francisco

KEY
● city
◉ country
- - - - - Sarunna's route

N
W ← → E
S

25

New Friends, New Words

1. **teacher** el maestro
2. **girl** la nĩna
3. **boy** el nĩno
4. **desk** el pupitre
5. **guitar** la guitarra
6. **map** el mapa
7. **clock** el reloj
8. **blackboard** la pizarra
9. **globe** el globo

26

At School
En la escuela

A

1	2	3	4	5
one	two	three	four	five
uno	dos	tres	cuatro	cinco
6	7	8	9	10
six	seven	eight	nine	ten
seis	siete	ocho	nueve	diez

10 **computer** la computadora

11 **computer disk** el disco

12 **ruler** la regla

13 **pencil** el lápiz

14 **book** el libro

15 **pen** la pluma

16 **calculator** la calculadora

17 **crayons** los creyones

18 **scissors** las tijeras

19 **easel** el caballete

28

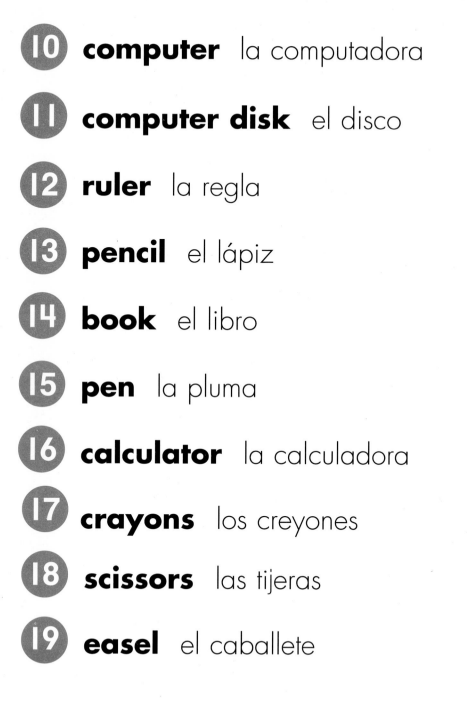

In the Classroom
En el salón de clases

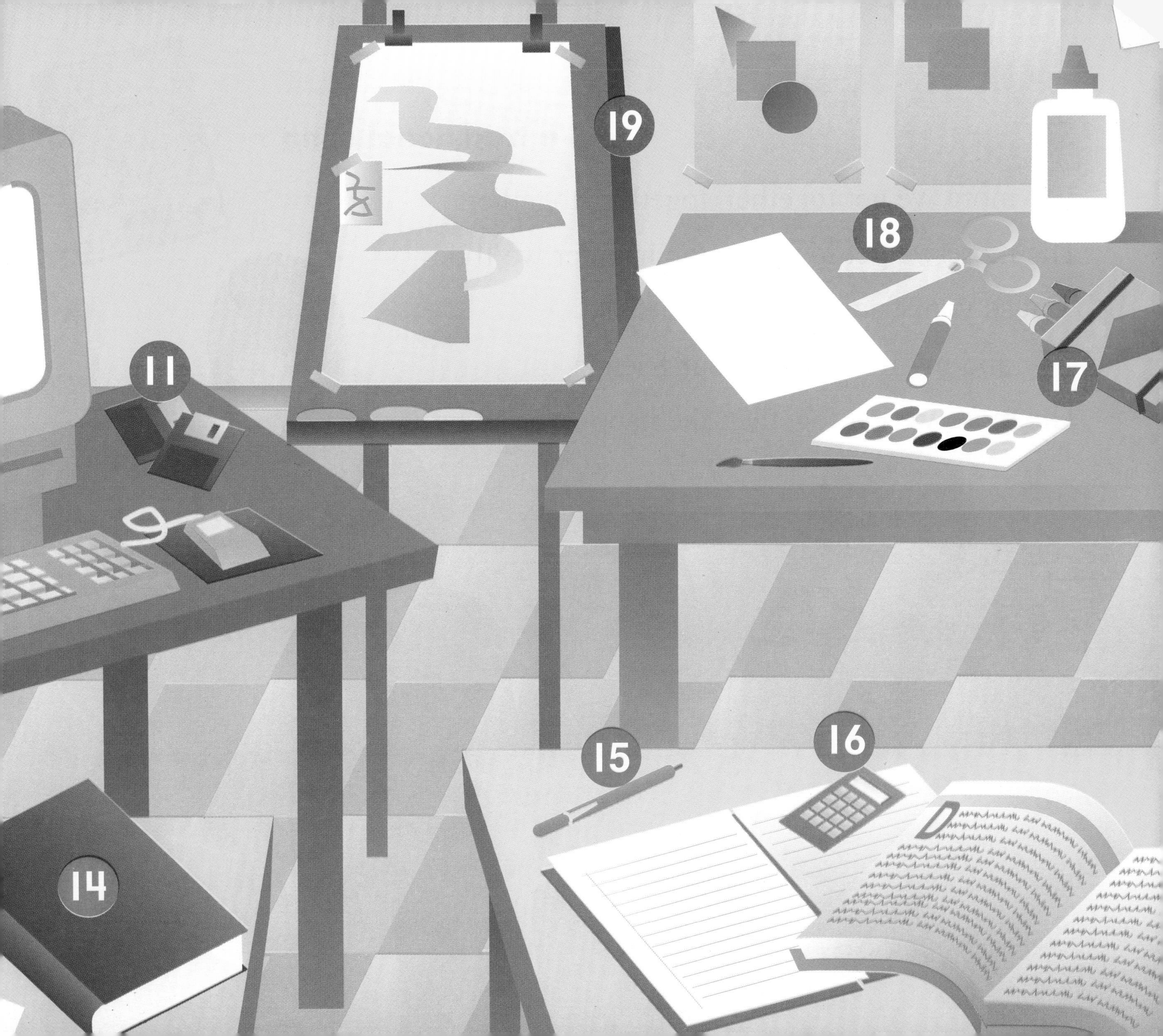

19
18
11
17
15
16
14

The More We Get Together

a traditional song

The more we get together, together, together,

The more we get together, the happier we'll be.

'Cause your friends are my friends,

   and my friends are your friends,

The more we get together, the happier we'll be.